CW01584072

The

Friargate Anthology

Creative Work from York Area Meeting Friends and Supporters

Edited by

Janet Dean
and
John Fieldhouse

This collection of poetry, prose, music and art has been contributed by members and supporters of the Quaker community in and around York. Funds raised from this Anthology will help to pay for the development of Friargate Quaker Meeting House as a community resource. We would like to thank everybody who gave their time and their work to this project. We received over sixty submissions of work from twenty five people, sufficient for at least a further Anthology and we are pleased that everybody who submitted work is represented here by at least one piece. Our thanks also to those buying the Anthology, as it is through you that we develop Friargate into a building that many more people can use and enjoy.

JD and JF, York 2015

© Janet Dean and John Fieldhouse

ISBN 978-1-904446-68-2

Printed and Published by
Quacks Books, 7 Grape Lane, Petergate
York YO1 7HU
t 01904 635967 f 01904623714

Acknowledgement

The editors are grateful to The Sessions Book Trust for a generous grant towards the publication costs of this book.

Cover Illustration
York Market - The Continuing Effect of History
Lois Folkard

Printed by offset lithography on 100gsm white paper.
Printed in Verdana font 12pt.

Contents

York Millennium Bridge by Brenda Tyler

Editors' Foreword

Where Does Writing Come From?

Or painting, or music, or any creative endeavour? How does it arise and how does it develop? These questions have been in my mind as we work on The Friargate Anthology, a collection of creative output in support of the development of Friargate Quaker Meeting House.

I started writing poetry as a young teenager when my subjects were folk singers and fox-hunting, social justice and caricatures of my friends; subsequently I wrote to deal with emotions, particularly those which arose around the time of the deaths of my parents when I was in my twenties. But I began to write more regularly after the birth of my son when he provided a constant stream of delightful imagery and I had some time off work to find space for writing.

My first published poem is one I have offered for the Anthology as it marks an early attempt to describe what it felt like to write. In About Writing (*Scarborough, Spring 1987*) I felt words forming as far off as waves out at sea, and although they built with the promise of originality and precise meaning, they often fell short, dissipating before I could get them on to the page.

For a long time I had believed that creativity had to arise in the form of inspiration, that ideas had to be allowed to bubble up before being pinned down and shaped into something meaningful or entertaining. This meant that my output was sparse, my creativity taking second place to the priorities of work and family life.

Over time, however, with the help of a string of creative writing tutors at the local library, residential courses and on the Master's in Creative Writing at York St John University, I have understood that creativity is a craft to learn, a skill to acquire.

Now, I believe, *I know*, that creativity comes from observation and listening, from making extensive notes in Moleskine squared-paper notebooks (a personal preference, not essential), from learning from others by reading, watching and hearing how they write, by discovering how to create your own stimuli for writing and ultimately by writing, writing, editing, editing, and writing, writing, writing.

I write now by drawing on internal resources – memory, reflection, post hoc analysis – and by using external triggers such as family history research, photographs, overheard stories and current events.

Quite recently I wrote *The Patient Ghost* which shows how differently I approach writing these days. It also shows how my writing has changed – most of what I write now reflects on my experience and feelings, is much more about personal commentary and contains layered messages rather than a straightforward idea. I am still able to read About Writing without too much embarrassment, but it is an arm's-length poem which uses the environment to describe an internal process rather than a reflection on personal growth, insight and the effects of grief.

I offer these thoughts as a consequence of a conversation with my co-editor John Fieldhouse and wonder what he thinks of my musings?

Janet Dean

Why Do I Write?

Janet's thoughtful words encourage my reflections toward the source of writing...and the inevitable questions arise, why do *I* write? How did it start? What do I like about writing, and what don't I like about it?

For me it all started late at night when I dropped a can of *spraymount* on the wood floor of my studio... Spraymount – you know, tsssz, tsssz, and you've got a nice gooey surface to stick things to. 'Things' being old bus tickets, cardboard, brown paper, tissue paper, newspaper; scraps headed for the recycle bin, only to be rescued and magicked into artistic creation.

It was my mother's voice coming from the room below which got me thinking. Heart disease is predictably unpredictable, and Mum had less than a year to live. Collage was no longer any good; I needed a quieter late night hobby, something that didn't involve wielding heavy pairs of scissors, the tearing of paper, the pacing up and down as I agonized over my work from impossible angles; the numerous washing's up, the mess.
Writing; yes I would try writing!

I was fifty nine, and, undeterred by the fact that I'd not produced a single piece of creative writing since school I made a stumbling start with five fumbling pieces. A three hundred and fifty page novel followed, it was crazy but I loved it. I was exploring a hitherto undiscovered facet of myself.

The transition from architectural designer to fiction writer was less bone-breaking than I thought it might be. "Quicker than the building business eh?" folk would comment. I had news for them, it's slower. Most short stories of mine have been around for at least a year before they make it into print. Writing's like making wine, you can't hurry it.

"Try and put it on one side for at least six months," my mentors and tutors advise me. "...Plan, prose, polish, publish; that's the sequence." There's an elegance and discipline about that phrase which I like.

"Ooooh, being a writer must be fun," enthuse people at parties. It's a great conversation piece – it can lead to all sorts I can tell you. Everybody reads, so everybody has some notion about writing which they are desperate to share with you.

What don't I like about writing? Very little deters me - just the odd tooth-grinding over those popular misconceptions.

"Is it autobiographical?" ask folk with a knowing look – as if they'd just witnessed you bumping an empty car in the office car park. The answer, from Ian McEwan right down to the humble amateur like me, is always the same; "Yes...but no." I mean just where do we writers get our material? Our heroes and villains are probably amalgams of everybody we've ever met. And that's where the trouble can start.

You make it into print. Your friends and relatives devour your work, proud to be associated with..."he's a published author now you know." Some time later you meet with those friends. Things seem odd. There are awkward silences, meaningful looks are exchanged, and it dawns on you that they think that they're in your story, parodied, pilloried, and vilified. Relationships can collapse – believe you me. At the other end of the scale there are those pals and kin who cry plaintively "we're really disappointed, we thought we'd be in there!" You can't win.

My writing does *not* provide me with a living. Perhaps one day, but for the present I give myself two simple guidelines:

i.) To be professional – in other words when I submit to an agent and they open the envelope they don't sigh loudly and throw the script over their left shoulder. ii.) To feel at the end of each month that I'm better than I was at its beginning.

Competitions – by definition - concentrate on a) beating your opponents, b) getting published. Nothing wrong with that, if you don't enter you can't win, but it can also help to keep your aims achievable. I see publication as a bonus, not as an end in itself. And there's always that nagging question, "When is a piece of writing finished?" Because when it's published – whether you like it or not – it is finished, frozen like an ice crystal, never to change...unlike its readers who still have their freedom. They are at liberty to read what they want, you as a successful writer must write what they want!

In the meantime I carry on producing plots, crafting characters, creating conflicts, wrestling with resolutions. Its five years since I dropped my can of spraymount and took up the pen, but you know I can't help thinking that writing has a strange similarity to collage. The old bus tickets, cardboard, brown paper, tissue paper, newspaper; scraps rescued from the recycle bin, only to be magicked into artistic creation.

Well, that's my story and I'm sticking to it!

John Fieldhouse

First retained for publication by Scribble Magazine in 2015

About Writing (Scarborough, Spring 1987)

A Thought comes like a wave,
far off by the edge
of the finger rocks,
swelling, unseen but perceptible
through some sense,
feeling which isn't touch,
like the knowledge of breathing

In the distance, unbroken,
a whole Thought,
faint and wordless,
growing as it rolls,
gaining strength and speed,
gathering sand, sea and debris;

but even in the middle distance
losing something, breaking off,
breaking down,
edges curling and spitting out
the foam of unwanted images,
only the centre strong and sure.

Here am I on the shore;
here my Thought comes,
climbing the sea steps
reaching, promising
crescendo,
longed for, hoped for and when
it crashes -
thunderous, wonderful, self-applauding,
but breaking short of the sea wall,
failing to reach me,
smashed before me,
sprayed unspeakable, unreadable,
unwritable.

Janet Dean

The Patient Ghost

Before I was a woman - I don't mean physically, I mean
consciously, in my mind - before that, I wrote a poem or two.
They were political poems; that was my stance.
As to where I was standing, I couldn't have said.

I went through that consciousness-raising, that debate
about the fate of women, and how oppressed we were.
I was not oppressed like my mother had been, but I felt it.
It was both liberation and load. Still is.

There is no evidence, nothing left from the hole of worst years;
all about death, all of the flesh, there was no mind.
Motherhood, that most womanly of acts, transmogrified me -
I became my mother.

Uneasily, we sit together, writing.
I try to make her write like Robert Frost, homespun and dark.
She waits, a patient ghost, nowhere to go.
I've got all the time in the world, she'll say.
Be still, let it come.

Janet Dean

First published in 2015. Commended Poem, Stanza Poetry Competition, judged by Jo Bell, on the theme of Darkness.

Nunnery Ruins on Iona

Here I sit.
Absorbing
four o'clock sunlight
rising beyond cloister gardens.
Rudimentary remains
of a refectory
open to wind and sky.
Gable ends against
brilliant firmament
broken
by drifting wisps of cloud.

Here lies
a crumbling thirteenth century
chapel
where long ago
Irish nuns
Lived
Slept
Ate and
Worshipped.
To the glory of God the Father.
or to Goddess the Mother?

Oh Sun!
Druid sun
yet granted place on Celtic cross.
You bring to life those blocks.
Red and grey stone
give way to deep shade
angling into
refectory wall.
Atop which
Plants weave gently
in the breeze.

In this chapel
Dedicated
to St. Mary the Virgin,
more than four centuries
of nuns
called it home.
Today
Its ruins are
Colourful
Warm.
Welcoming

Margy Vernon

EVE

Eve didn't mean to fall in love with the serpent. Ever since emerging from Adam's side and metamorphosing from a very ordinary looking rib into a full grown woman in her early 20's, she had been a dutiful cavewife. Eve was not what you would call beautiful, but on the other hand, neither was she ugly. She was 5'5" in her skin boots, weighed 8 stone and measured in at 34", 25", 36", quite normally proportioned one might say. She had long black hair, brown eyes, and an olive complexion. While not exactly house proud, Eve did keep the cave free of the flotsam and jetsam of life; bones, nut shells, plum stones, out-of-fashion animal skins and the like.

The trouble with Eve was that she craved company, any kind of company other than dull, humourless old Adam and wrathful, capricious, humourless God. Adam often scolded her for not showing proper respect for their illustrious Creator, but Eve paid little attention. She was always a bit contemptuous of Adam's grovelling attitude toward the Old Man in the Sky.

To make matters even worse between Eve and her husband they didn't really fancy each other. At least Eve didn't fancy Adam. His feelings were never easy to interpret.

The serpent, on the other hand, fascinated Eve. S/he (of indeterminate gender) was both witty and wise, sensitive to Eve's moods and feelings, knowledgeable about many things, fun loving, and very sexy. To make a long story short, Eve had an affair of sorts with the serpent. I'm not sure if it was a real affair, but they did eat an apple together and later Eve even persuaded Adam to join in the fun.

God was not pleased. Not so much by the apple as by Eve refusing to consummate her marriage to Adam. Eve, with the help of the serpent, put up a lively defense. Their case was based on the premise that being physically a part of Adam, his own rib in fact, Eve had simply been avoiding the sin of incest. But God expelled them all from the Garden anyway and life has been unfair ever since.

Margy Vernon

In This Together

You broke the rules that morning and rode over
the dew-fresh grass of the common. Warm in Lycra,
thighs strong, man-bag bulging – keys, towel, new trunks
(a size smaller after all this exercise) –
you pedalled fast, past scented limes and London planes
stretching in the seven o'clock sun; imagined

The stoop of the heron in the pond behind,
its dive an ugly elegance; looked forward
to honing your own diving skills, streamlining
through that Hockney-blue brilliance, thirsty
for the bitter shock that freezes the mind when
toes have barely left the white of the tiles and
high-summer's rustle in the dappling trees
becomes a liquid gurgle pumping in your ears.

A small crowd, not an orderly queue, disturbed
like bees; the kiosk attendant – eyebrows raised,
shoulders shrugged – her body pronouncing words that
her migrant's tongue, as yet, could not. Through a gap
you glimpsed the surface, gleaming, almost in reach.

But I've come a long way! A very long way!
Shrug. *What about my children? Been coming here*
for years! Shrug. *It's an absolute disgrace!* Shrug.
Is this what we fought two world wars for? Eyebrows.

CLOSED FOR A PRIVATE EVENT.

That bitter shock. *Private.* On the kind of day
when you just want to go for an open-air swim,
grow numb the longer you're in, each hundred yards
a chest-punching challenge, the Lido's waters
like communal treasure, a century deep.

Two children looked from the face of their mother
to the head in the kiosk, as if to say
Adults, fix this, now. You turned away. How to
reclaim, unlock this day? By the pond you fought
to control your breath and caught the heron's lift,
wings prehistoric, slow, slow, as if it knew,
had always known and had the key to it all.

Yvie Holder

Bicycling On the Moors

Slowly, pedalling mostly, but pushing
on the steep bits, I climb onto the moor.
Sentinels, rooks stand by their nests,
shiny in bare watchtowers; a hare
sits in a field, and higher, larks rise
from the heather and tufted grass,
choralling madly in the eye of the sun.

Along the ridge, wind ruffles tormentil,
and marked stones and unmarked tumuli
stud the moor with lost importance. Below, farms,
knots at the junctions of hedge and wall
stitch the fields together, and the crazy clack
of tractors warps and woofs the land.

This is not Paradise – a barn sags ruined;
a kestrel darts low, and fatal; the windows
of village shop, school and pub are blind;
a crow picks eyes from a dying rabbit.

This is the country. How it became so
is a story we could discover – glaciers and wind and water,
man's digging and chopping, ploughing and shaping,
his need for constant movement, for shelter, food,
and quietly, unbeknown to the makers, to manufacture beauty.

It is what we have made it:
the cities, fields, and forests bear our mark.
We have worked with the Earth;
beauty and utility are in the blood,
and we have sometimes shown respect, and love
for what surrounds us – traits that may save us yet.
This is the practice to follow, the promise to keep.

John Gilham
First published in 'Learning to Breathe' by Stairwell Books, 2015

Tour De France

I'm glad I didn't miss it.

For here were streets where on every shop
was a yellow bicycle,
where the butcher touted poulet, porc, and saucisson,
where berets bloomed on many a head
and bunting spanned the road
from deli to quincaillerie.

I'm glad I didn't miss it.

The hoopla, the mafficking
the carefully staged build up
while the crowds got thicker,
and the barriers took the strain.

We cheered everything:
the caravan, as it hurled out freebies,
officials in their dark cars,
the mayor in his limo,
and old ladies cycling to church.
We even cheered policemen
and the gendarmerie.
How strange is that ?!

I'm glad I didn't miss it.

Even though when they came,
they were gone in a burst of colour,
of helmets, of brown legs and arms,
of wild cheering, mad photography,
people on tiptoe, people on ladders,
people on stepstools, people
on balconies and walls.
People, maybe, who don't cycle
or even own a bike.

I'm glad I didn't miss it.

It was like having the World Cup
At the end of your street,
Wimbledon in the local park,
the parade of the gladiators or the running of the bulls
within an arms reach.

Bravo Yorkshire. Vive Le Tour.

John Gilham

The Bonfire of the Vanities

Lydia loved working at Compact Theatre. She loved the girls; monosyllabic Cynth, booming m'Anne Mountain, twinkly Dark Svelte Julie, cheeky Dame Monique. She loved the boys – the mysterious and ambivalently named Tess. She even quite liked the directors Kim and Noj; so it seemed all the more hateful when Noj said he didn't like her work.

It was her first job as Set Designer - *The Crucible.* Would you believe it? *The Crucible* had been her final project at college. The tutors had held a competition and it was her design which had come first. So that's the one that got built, and the whole year group had worked on it.

Noj wanted a bonfire on *his* set. Lydia couldn't remember one, but Noj said that anything to do with witches and executions would need a bonfire. Lydia racked her brains and came up with what she thought was a good idea.

It was a double helix in red and orange acetate. The bottom ends of the ribbons were steel-wired to a timber board which rested on the stage floor. When a crew member pulled down on the contraption, the shiny double helix would quiver and dance up and down. Lit from below it looked just like the sparks of an angry bonfire. Of course on the night there would be smoke guns, and with audio soundtrack of hissing and spitting it would be fantastic.

'Darling I hate it. I hate, hate, hate it!' Noj minced up and down in the blackness of the studio. Lydia felt an awful pang of adrenaline.

'It's symbolic.'

'Shambolic more like.'

'It'll look great on the night.'

'We need something more literal. *'Cru'* isn't a modern play. It's got to look like what it is...it's got to smoulder more than spark. This looks like something out of the window of a Gas showroom. In fact if you want to know dahling, it's an effing pig's ear!'

What he was saying was unfair, unkind. He was just going through a bad time with Kim. Lydia felt like bursting into tears there and then. But Lydia never did anything in a hurry. She dismantled the bonfire, tidied its composite parts into the props cupboard; packed away all her personal things. Then, before returning to her digs she went and ate a lonely and tearful meal in a Chinese restaurant.

The next day was Saturday. Of course, the company all worked but Lydia did not go in to work. They could all stew - or smoulder whatever the case may be. She got the bus in as usual, but instead of her normal stop at John Walton Street she got off near the cathedral, hurried past the School of Music, along Hunts Bank, into the railway station where she bought a ticket to Haworth. She'd always wanted to go there.

It was late May. Somewhere there was sun, but only a small percentage of its lux was penetrating the mist which hung over the town. The air smelt damp. Gloom; that's why she'd come; to absorb and be absorbed into the desolation, the cheerlessness, the melancholy, the sombre, the heavy-heartedness, the funereal... There was no shortage of adjectives, or nouns to describe the way she was feeling.

Lydia was surprised how few folk there were in Haworth. All right it was a bit misty, but it was 'season'. She went round the Parsonage, the church, looked at the Hawthorn Enclosure; peered through the windows of the Black Bull. She got talking to some Swedish people, could hear German being spoken, and there were a lot of Japanese folk around. Mum had said that the Brontes were now 'bigger in Japan than in Britain'...but that still didn't seem to explain why it was so quiet.

She remembered her mum close to tears after reading an account of how Charlotte Bronte took her sister Anne to Scarborough. The article said that they'd stayed in York on the way, and Charlotte had wheeled Anne round York Minster in a borrowed chair. Anne's arms were so thin they were like little sticks, her cheeks worn away. Anne had asked to go to evensong but the doctor said 'no'. The family had thought that Scarborough would make her well. Anne and Charlotte arrived there all right, but next day Anne died.

By now Noj's hissy-fit over Lydia's bonfire seemed a long way away. She went to the post office, bought a picture post card and wrote it with her new gel pen.

Hello Mum & Dad
Guess what? I'm in Haworth. It's very quiet here...

'Why so quiet?' she asked the man in the post office. He had lovely eyebrows which stuck out at the sides, like the ears of an eagle owl. They were double; one horizontal bush of hair, the other pair rising at forty five degrees.

'Has't th'not 'eard of t'Cup Final lass?'

He moved closer as she held out the card ready for stamping.

'Hast thou not heard?' He boomed in a terrifying baritone, like an Old Methody minister seeking out truants from chapel.

Of course, football, the Holy Grail! She felt like a shirker, a laggard, worse still an unbeliever, a heathen. Of course, you had to bow down didn't you? Worship, share triumphs, weep upon one another's shoulders, swap trivia, punch air. What an error! She had fled from humiliation, and would now have to return to a greater one.

'Do you know, she went to Haworth on Cup Final Day!'

John Fieldhouse

Fossil Hunter

Beneath a slatted grey sky
We walked on Runswick beach
Giant stones from another age keeping the metallic sea at bay
The echoes of fossil hunters' hammers
Ruffling the edges of the still lazy afternoon.

A woman at the base of a small rock fall
Deftly split the shale
And there in the coiled ruts
Lay revealed the secrets of that pre-Biblical era
A visitor to these shores when the sky was shot with a more crimson hue.

As though awakened from a dream-filled sleep
Ewe stopped and stared and marvelled;
That moment in time when the unknown, but yearned for mystery
Comes into being.

'This rock's too big to carry-I'll have to make it smaller.'
And so saying she chipped away
And broke the ammonite.
Laughing she said, 'I'll have to stick it at home with my special glue.'

Beneath the rock strewn cliff
The foam of the last wave to reach the shore
Seeped into the sand and with it
The suspended moment.

The careless foot that crushes the seed.
The storm that wrecks the boat. The earth that overheats-
These unintended consequences of which our lives are made.

In a single moment, our hands distracted by wanton purpose,
We desecrate that which most deserves our respect.
The sacred held in that ancient find
Touches us, and in the touching-
Shatters in our clumsy embrace.

And we, children of the present,
Mourn its passing and search for it still.

Barbara Webb

The Good Doctor

(For Colin Liew, consultant, University College Hospital, London)

When at last you got the news
That took you over the cliff edge
Into the black crevasse of all that's feared-
Loss of children, future, the ordinary rich pleasures
Of this difficult life, and your spirits sank
In the cold currents of a black lake.

Then came the good doctor
Whose calm can settle a ward
As when a harsh wind drops
Or evening sun breaks through.
His careful explanations settled you.
No ego flaunts itself, no phoney cheerfulness,
Just sense, and human kindness
And time in a driven life
To lean on windowsills and chat.
On his instruction treatment changes,
The right drug's given, a weekend out
To breathe the air on Hampstead heath
And see the leaves and foolish dogs
And rediscover all the things you are
Besides a woman who is going to die
Before she thought.
All this the good doctor brings
And his mysterious inward smile
Expressing more than understanding.

Angela Fisher 2010 (1944-2011)

Contributed by Barbara Webb

A Trilogy

Coming Out

It's peekaboo
From behind a mask.
Now you see me,
Then you don't.
When I see you,
I won't look.

Fleeting moments,
Eyes and words,
Souls connect,
My heart awakes,
Inch by inch
Laid bare.

My coming out
Is a dance with you.
Tiny steps,
To and fro,
Through the dark
To daylight.

My Inner Shed

My inner shed
Has tubes of paint
To squirt and mix
And swirl and fix.

The paper dries,
The next sheet waits,
Spread out to see
Or just to be.

Or maybe words
Are best today,
To play with rhyme
And name my time.

I rove around
The treasure trove,
And choose with care,
Prefer it spare.

I love this way
To speak my heart,
How great if it
Is also art!

Coming home

My scattered self,
Flung asteroid wide,
Is coming home.
Magnet drawn
By quiet,
Patient,
Quick-eyed love.

Carol Ann Hooper

Yellow Mandala by Rosie Gray

The Leeds Carol.
Tune: 'In the bleak midwinter' by Gustav Holst.

1. Long ago when Mary
found herself with child,
Mary's Mum was shattered
Mary's Dad went wild.
How could she have let them down?
Who could be the man?
Mary was in trouble
in that far off land.

2. Joseph seemed the culprit,
but it was not he.
So says holy scriptures:
virtuous was she.
So they were to marry soon,
yearning to be one.
Love and human longings
could have made their son.

3. Later on Saint Luke told
stories to define
how the son of Mary
came to be divine.
How the Holy Spirit had
caused the child to grow,
how the virgin Mary
never man did know.

4. Much was made of Mary,
gentle, meek and mild,
how she was unblemished
bore this God-like child.
Fully human, son of man
fully God as well.
How his life and dying
saved us all from Hell.

5. Doubts about his father
never fully went.
Joseph took them on when
God an angel sent.
Could it be a Roman man
who had raped the maid?
Was she violated?
Quite a common fate.

6. Violated virgin,
nothing new at all.
Long before and after
many women's fall.
Could it be that Mary has
messages for us?
Victim and survivor
who transformed her loss?

7. Glory be to Mary,
well she raised her son.
Honour due to Joseph,
who did take them on.
Shame upon the Roman chap
If it was his seed.
(spoken) BUT
Good can come from evil,
Even such a deed.

Ruth Lissner Corry

Child's Chair at Swarthmoor

Fell's fifth sits still in her highly polished chair.
Three years fill the seat, hands rest upon the wood.
A gentle curve supports her arms. Back straight,
head held high and true. Feet neat upon the boards.

Quiet as visitors climb the outside stair, she waits
in Fell's parlour. She does not tug her bonnet bows,
fidget while they tarry. She has already learnt to hold
inner stillness in her heart; does not fret at rules

that bring her family peace. The solid door
opens with a steady tread, a smile descends,
fixes her attention. Her concentration breaks -

"Granddad, please play ball with me."

Richard Carpenter

RIEVAULX ABBEY

White-robed men of long ago:
Stone by stone, they built Rievaulx
As part of their vocation.

Fluted columns rising high,
Windows arching to the sky,
Harmonious formation.

No monks now to heed the chime
Calling worshippers to prime,
Or cloistered mediation.

Tourists marvel at the view,
Wagtails run and pigeons coo -
No other congregation.

Yet the grandeur of its scale
Dominating wooded vale
Is still an inspiration.

Elisabeth Alley

Why I am a Quaker

I joined the society when I was nearly sixty, now almost twenty-five years ago. I have moved during much of my life with academics, the majority of whom are either agnostics or, more frequently, indifferent to the claims of religion. This continued the trend of my previous life; agnostic parents, no religious education in youth in school or elsewhere, little acquaintance with religious people. I regarded myself as an agnostic until I fell under the influence of a friend of aggressive atheist views, and for long called myself an atheist too. I do so no longer.

In place of religion I became a political zealot, a process not encouraged by my rather alarmed parents. Readers will have heard of the loony left; this is a description of myself which I do not regret, indeed regard rather as a badge of honour. Being a slow learner I have never changed my political views.

But things do change. Left-wing politics in this country has become over the decades less a matter of principle, more a question of which expedient is likely to lead to electoral success. It is hard to blame professional politicians for this behaviour; their careers are at stake. This is not the case with outsiders. I reached a point at which I concluded that politics was for politicians a matter of priorities not amenable to periodic public pressure, in short that political activism was little more than a cover for a small group of highly placed men and women determined to pursue their own agenda

There were straws in the wind. I attended the Quaker-founded Swarthmore College near Philadelphia where I participated in meetings held by the liberal Student Christian Movement. I attended meeting for worship occasionally (there was a meeting house on the campus) and though Quakerism did not 'take', I never lost interest in the religion. When I became a university teacher I gradually came to realise how much British society and the nascent labour movement owed to their Christian roots, as much (in the case of the labour movement) organisationally as ideologically. I came too to understand that the various Christian churches had not been at least from the mid or later nineteenth century a single 'Tory Party at prayer'; but that social reform more often than not came from Christian roots and the Christian social conscience. (I did not and do not ignore the fact that the history of Christianity is scarred by war, persecution and a metamorphosis from 'the sentiment of a heartless world' to the indispensable ally of power.) In this context it is worth noting that one of the most influential social reformers of his generation, Seebohm Rowntree, was not only a Quaker but a York Quaker and a prominent member of our own meeting.

So early in 1991, when the British government was about to join the Americans in enthusiastically attacking Iraq at the start of the first Gulf War, and the Labour Party dared not stand out against them, my wife and I happened to walk past Friargate meeting house. There in a window was pasted a streamer with the message: 'Quakers oppose all war'. (A similar streamer with the same message now adorns our own home.) The next day we attended meeting for worship and have done so almost weekly ever since. We appreciated our reception and I have never forgotten the numerous visitors and heartening messages which reached me when I spent eleven weeks in hospital in 2001. But my adhesion to Quakerism is not founded on my personal reception, though the reality of a Quaker community has certainly been no hindrance. I appreciate silent worship and occasional spoken ministry. I am not a mystic but anyone can see that a worshipping community is greater than the sum of its individual parts; that a 'gathered meeting' is a reality, not just a phrase. I endorse the Quaker testimonies and have a special loyalty to pacifism and (to descend to relative trivia) the absence of titles. Above all, perhaps, I appreciate our absence of creed and that while our denomination has descended from firm Christian roots, we do not insist that members and attenders pass a test of their beliefs. While most would unhesitatingly call ourselves Christians, there is room also for those whose religious beliefs are unformed or sceptical. I add that while inconsistencies are easy to find in the New Testament ('Jesus is an ayatollah' declares my atheist friend), the principal message as regards our fellow human beings is one of equality and love. For a European or anyone educated in the European tradition some form of Christianity, the religion with which our history is impregnated, is a natural faith. And there are many forms from which to choose. Some are as repugnant to me as they are to any atheist who seeks to tar all Christians with the brush of fundamentalism.

I stress the fact that I have never thought of Quakerism as a political organisation or sought to use it for political ends. I am, however, convinced as many Quakers have been before me and are today, that religion and politics are complementary and that collective commitment to particular issues (though not to particular political parties) is not to be avoided.

Some years ago I told a group of Anglicans that I believed that the Quaker religion was 'a religion for grown-ups'. It was a crass statement to make before that group and I am embarrassed to think that I made it. Yet it is certainly what I believe. We have principles not subject to political expediency. We do not have priests to tell us what to believe, much less 'bishops to show [us] the way' as Flanders and Swann sang long ago. Most Quakers are serious-minded people with a serious interest in reforming the world about them. While our record of equal rights for women and men during our nearly four hundred-year history is by no means as unblemished as some of us like to think, it is superior to most if not all other churches. Our latter-day espousal of equality in matters of sexual orientation is one of which to be proud and our denomination was among the first to support marriage between people of the same sex.

I have criticisms. Our emphasis on consideration for all views inhibits decision-making, sometimes fatally. Too many Friends seem to have little interest in anything Quaker other than 'being quiet on a Sunday morning', as a veteran Quaker once complained to me. Our emphasis on all days being equally holy so that every day is Christmas day, for example, means that some Quakers feel that there is no need to do anything specific in practice. (Observing Lent at least ensures that one does do something in commemoration of one's faith.) There is a danger both of self-flagellation and of complacency. ('I know that there is horrifying injustice in the world but think of the flowers that bloom in the spring!') There is a danger too of being for everything and against nothing. (The aggression and certainty of George Fox's day has given way to reluctance to condemn views one does not hold, a by no means wholly unworthy development,) But these are the almost inevitable defects of our virtues. Taken as a whole Quakerism is the most satisfying faith which has come my way. The world, particularly but by no means only the English-speaking world, needs Quakerism, and our declining numbers are a matter of serious concern. I need Quakerism. I shall attend meeting for worship so long as I am physically able and I expect to remain a Quaker until my death.

David Rubinstein

Meeting for Worship

From word-filled foyer
Through a shuffling of settling
To a quietly lengthening loosening
Of mind-ties, heart-cramps, stubborn anxieties -
Freed of maelstrom, down we are drawn
To a stilling, a waiting,
A word-free centre.

There then at last,
World-spell gently broken,
The watery depth does not drown us.
It slips from our grasp, will not be commanded,
Yet it holds us, surrounds us.
Supporting, it guides our gaze,
Points us beyond.

Beyond knowing
To unknowing.
From grasp
To trust.
From fear
To love.

Barbara Windle

Oh Where Are We Going?

Musings on a March Ministry closely based on Auden's *'Oh Where are you Going?'*

'Oh where are you going?' said Sneerer to Saver
'The path that you follow is only a lie.
Yonder's the grave that just leads to grieving;
Eternal life is just pie in the sky.'

'I know where I'm going.' said Saver to Sneerer
'There's only one path that can ever be right.
The sin in you heart will lead you to hurting,
Where's there's no heaven there's just endless night.'

'Oh which way to follow?' said Quailer to Quaker
'The ways are a labyrinth; there's no way to know.
All paths are in darkness and so full of danger.
The routes are so many: just where do we go?'

'You must find your true path.' said Quaker to Quailer
'For anyone else's cannot be your own.
'Your spark that is lit joins with multiple lights,
And together, yet separate, we'll find our way home.'

Kate Vernon-Rees

Four Poems

1. What I'm becoming..

With age, fears's a waxing moon;
My heart a tumbleweed boat on black Ocean,
Drifting, one-oared, aimless..
Dreams distant, frail dust in a strong wind..
Soul shrunken, old sand under stone..

But life grinds me finer as I grow,
A reed in the wind, shaken but strong;
A leaf in the air, free-flying..
Slow alchemy is grappling with me,
Inner light is shining..
Home is within; my heart's a door,
My life a wheel, still rolling..

Facet by facet, grit on bone,
I'm a diamond half polished,
A diamond near done...
A small Rock , turned at last to the sun...

2. April, that year

Small dark quiet space,
A branching, reaching, fingering
Of roots, a stretch of stem;
Sap is rising - stirring seed, budding tree...

Slow, relentless,unstoppable, sweet as air...
Old as time,
Blossom sketched against bark;
Fragmentary blooms suddenly full..
Caught in becoming, soon gone.
Watch it soar, spring...rolling, reeling;
Fragile as the flowers it births, scatters,
Then treads upon...

3. I swing, buffeted,
By this wind, my life.
Heaving small footprints,
Hiccuping in the sun..
The air is still, sweet, green
If I choose
And the blinkers are off...
Towards evening now
In this long day-
A row of new mornings
Still lie unexplored;
With any potential
I may choose; or none.
Beads on a rope , taking shape..
This necklace I never planned
Is finally fitting
My neck.
It's' lustre makes me proud.
I have worn, longtime;
A lot of dusty pebbles.
Pearls, they are now..
Grown with grace and grit...

4. Earth was bearing
The trees away.
Pointing flowers; throws of colour;
Travelling, each of us, all the scented directions..
Spun held me, fixed in a burning birth;
Whilst the air blew acute angles
Around daisies.
Birds cried their lives into branches
Green with a day's tenancy.
Clouds frowned at Me , dissolving my dust.
Does the stem know of
It's hanging spider?
The sky bend to greet
Each waxing moon?
We are so small.
Our hearts beat hugely

Against clay rows
Of these particular days.
Each one a bead on a string.
We are numbered.
Our tomorrow's hang; spiders
On the stem of heaven.
A real world to be in;
I have given myself.

Linda Baker

The Tiny Little Girl and the Great Big Robot

Once upon a time, there was a tiny little girl. She lived in a tiny little room, in the middle of a great big robot. She had always lived inside the robot. She had no memory of getting into it, or of any kind of life outside it.

The tiny little room was very pretty. It had pictures of flowers on the walls, and soft carpet, as green as grass. The ceiling was a bright sky blue. It was always at the perfect temperature, and from time to time a soft breeze wafted through, freshening the air, and bringing a smell like pine trees.

The tiny little girl was quite comfortable in her room. She had books, and music, and boxes of yarn to crochet. If she got bored, there was a magic window through which she could watch stories about other great big robots. She was not happy, but she was content.

The tiny little girl never dreamed that her life could be any different. She had always been a tiny little girl inside a great big robot, and that was the way things would always be.

One day, the tiny little girl woke up feeling very odd. She felt sad. No, that wasn't it - she felt angry. Angry and sad. And hopeless. Angry, sad and hopeless.

She wanted to stay in bed and do nothing, and yet she felt she had to be moving, doing something, anything. But none of the things she thought of doing felt like the right thing.

She sat in the middle of the grass-green carpet and burst into tears. She drummed her tiny little heels on the floor, and battered it with her tiny little fists, and screamed and shouted. Nothing made her feel any better. She flopped back on the grass-green carpet, chest heaving, whining softly. Her tiny little fists clenched and unclenched, and her whole body was rigid with misery and frustration.

Her fingers brushed against something smooth and hard on the soft carpet. She opened her swollen eyes and saw that it was a key. Not a fancy golden key, covered with mystical etchings or encrusted with precious stones. Just a plain, utilitarian key.

She turned it over in her hand, completely confused. Where had it come from? And what did it unlock? She dried her eyes and stood up, turning slowly on the spot to look for something that the key might fit.

In one corner of the room, she saw a door. Where had that come from? Surely it had not been there before today. The tiny little girl was certain that she had never seen it before. And yet there it was, the same colour as the walls, looking as if it had always been part of the room.

Slowly, and rather unwillingly, the tiny little girl moved closer to the door. It was smooth and featureless, and did not look special at all. The tiny little girl decided that it could not possibly lead anywhere exciting, because it was so plain and unprepossessing. It was just an ordinary door, with a brass doorknob and a keyhole.

The tiny little girl decided to try the key in the keyhole. What harm could it do? This was not a special, magic door, after all. She put the plain, flat key into the keyhole of the plain, flat door, and twisted it. There was a sharp click, and the door swung open.

For a moment, the tiny little girl was blinded. Golden light flooded the doorway, warm and glowing and beautiful. The tiny little girl took a step forward, and found herself on a golden spiral staircase. Step by step, she slowly ascended the staircase, wondering where on earth it could be leading.

At the top of the staircase was a broad platform.

The tiny little girl stepped onto it, and found herself standing in front of two enormous round windows. With great apprehension, she peeped out of one of the windows. She could not believe what she saw.

Through the window, she could see green grass. Not a carpet, like the one in her room, nothing that was just the colour of grass. She recognised it from the stories she had seen through the magic window, the stories she had thought were only make-believe.

She could see real flowers, too, and a real blue sky. How could that be? She backed away from the windows. Suddenly she knew where she was. High above her room, with two enormous round windows? She must be right up inside the head of the great big robot.
Strange emotions started to fizz inside her - excitement, happiness, fear. She was out of her own tiny little room, in a great big place she had never dreamed of going. It was all too much. She slid to the floor, and everything went black.

When she woke up, she was lying on her back, bathed in an enfolding warmth. There was a soft, tickly floor beneath her, and a wonderful smell of flowers and pine trees. She stretched luxuriantly, like a cat, and slowly opened her eyes.

She was outside.

No longer looking through the eyes of the robot, she was seeing it all for herself for the first time.

Gingerly, she sat up and looked down at herself. Her knees didn't look quite right. She drew up her skirt, and gasped in surprise. They were not her knees, of flesh and blood. They were robot knees.

She stumbled to her feet in a panic. Was she now a robot too? What had happened? Who had turned her from a tiny little girl into a tiny little robot?

As she looked, her robot body began to soften and turn pink. The robot joints dissolved into bone and muscle, and the shiny metal became plump and smooth, with fine downy hairs. The angular robot face developed cheekbones and lips, eyebrows and eyelashes, and the metallic curls merged into waves of real hair. The tiny little girl touched her new face. She was crying.
Now she understood what had happened. She had not been turned into a robot. For the first time, she was properly inhabiting the robot, bringing it fully to life. She was the great big robot, and she was the tiny little girl, and the two were one.

She felt an unaccustomed surge of joy. She would no longer be shut up in the tiny little room. She had the whole world to play in.

She threw back her head and laughed at the bright blue sky, and the green grass, and the beautiful flowers, and the pine trees. She turned around on the spot, taking in her new world, and how beautiful it was.

Then she couldn't stay still any longer. Laughing and crying, skipping and jumping, the real live girl began to run.

Heather Cawte

In happy memory of Anne Reynolds, David Gray, Marion Owen, Humphrey Terry and many other Friargate Friends

Fox's Round

George Fox

ANDREW CARTER

Andante ♩. = a valiant 60

© Andrew Carter 2015

13
ev - 'ry - one, ev - 'ry - one. Walk cheer - ful - ly o - ver the world,
cheer - ful - ly o - ver the world, walk cheer - ful - ly,
walk cheer - ful - ly, ans - wer - ing that of God in
ans - wer - ing that of God in ev - 'ry - one, ev - 'ry - one,
17
walk cheer - ful - ly, ans - wer - ing that of God in
ans - wer - ing that of God in ev - 'ry - one, ev - 'ry - one,
ev - 'ry - one, ev - 'ry - one,
21
ev - 'ry - one, ev - 'ry - one, in ev - - 'vry - one.
f
in ev - - 'vry - one.
in ev - - 'vry - one.
in ev - - 'vry - one.

La Mer

The mother rocks you gently,
salt tears bearing you up
in lightness and freedom.
Soft waves caress and hold you
as you start to swim.

Then, as a mother urges her child
to independence,
the ocean pushes and tosses you
ever nearer your destiny on shore.

As you reach sand you smile
in gratitude,
knowing that she'll always be there.

Nicky Metcalfe

A Story of Courage and a Miraculous Rescue

retold by Mabel Weiss

(Mabel Weiss was a resident at Lamel Beeches, York and this piece was printed some years ago in their Christmas Newsletter)

Before the war I taught Bess at Parliament Hill School in London. Her parents decided to send her and her brother to Canada under a Government-sponsored evacuation scheme but, as Bess relates so graphically, the ship was torpedoed in mid-Atlantic. After her rescue Bess sent the most moving account of this terrible experience and the subsequent miraculous rescue in a letter to the school. That letter is now in the archives of the Imperial War Museum. This considered account was written sixty years later after she had taken part in numerous radio and TV interviews. Indeed, it was hearing her being interviewed by Brian Redhead on a Today programme that helped some of us who had taught her to get in touch with her again. The BBC gave us her address and we had a very happy reunion.

It was a wild, grey day that dawned on 18th September 1940 in London. The night had been full of the noises of war. Explosions, crashing buildings, raging fires, all part of the experiences of those who lived in the shadow of the Blitz. Now, with the coming of the dawn, with yellow streaks in the grey sky, came too the steady and insistent sound to the 'All Clear', telling weary Londoners that, just for a while, life could be resumed in a hollow kind of normality until darkness arrives, and with it, the Luftwaffe.

In their North London home, Rosina and Bernard Walder thanked God that their two children were safe from such alarms, and were, by now beginning their new lives in Canada. They has parted from their children with great courage – and hidden tears – sending them off to the safety and peace of a caring and welcoming home for the duration of the war. Their children, Louis, aged nine, and Bess, aged fifteen, had sailed from Liverpool on Friday 13th September on board the luxurious and elegantly designed flagship of the Ellerman line, the City of Benares, bound for Halifax, Nova Scotia. The beautiful ship, with all her crew, had been commissioned by the Children's Overseas Evacuation Board – a Government-sponsored scheme- to take 90 children from vulnerable areas to new wartime homes in Canada. In addition to the evacuees were other passengers, ten of whom were children travelling with their parents.

What Rosina and Bernard could not know when they talked together about their children over breakfast that morning, was that their youngsters, far from being safe, were in mortal danger. The liner had been torpedoed in mid-Atlantic – 700 miles from the coast of Ireland – during the night of 17th September in a raging gale. Their daughter, Bess, was adrift in mid-ocean on an upturned lifeboat and their son was on a fragile raft. The prospect of rescue for either child was remote.

Each child was well aware that the other was likely either to have drowned or perhaps have been fatally injured by the explosion. They, by now, had seen many such deaths of children and adults alike. During that terrible night, a very deep Atlantic depression brought a Force 9 gale to add to the havoc and horror of shipwreck. The beautiful ship that had given its passengers so much comfort and pleasure had sunk within 30 minutes with its Captain on board. Most of the passengers which had been lucky enough to find places in the few lifeboats that had been launched successfully found themselves sitting in water up to their chests, mountainous seas waterlogging the boats. Soon they too foundered. An extremely fortunate few, still alive, clung desperately to anything that could float, hoping that somehow they might soon be rescued. In most cases it was a forlorn hope.

Bess' lifeboat had been launched the right way up, but because of the angle of the sinking ship the davits were unable to control the boat as it plunged down into the ocean. It filled with water and soon capsized, throwing all the passengers down into the wild and terrible water. Bess – a strong swimmer who had been taught by her father to swim in the sea – surfaced, and as she did so, felt her hands touch the side of the upturned lifeboat. She clung on to the ropes that encircled the boat, gradually inching her way upwards to grasp the keel with both hands. Alongside her were others who had done the same, including another girl whose hands now were opposite her own, also clinging to the keep. Her name was Beth, and the two girls spoke briefly, communication being difficult in those conditions.

Beth, Bess and an Indian seaman were now the only survivors of all those who first boarded the lifeboat. The two girls clung on throughout that dreadful night, battered, bruised and almost knocked senseless by the enormous waves being whipped up into a frenzy by the gales. Their bodies were numb with cold, tongues swollen and their mere existence precarious in the extreme. The only way that they could keep from sliding into the ferocious sea was by clinging on to the keel of the upturned lifeboat – 'clinging on like grim death.'

The Indian seaman had tied himself to the rudder of the boat by one of the ropes. This kept his head out of the water but he was already delirious with fear and cried out desperately for rescue, praying aloud to Allah. As the terrible night went on, both girls, almost unable to speak to one another now, had a strong motivation to survive. Bess needed to get back to explain to her parents what had happened to her brother Louis who, by now, she was certain, had drowned. Beth wanted to return to her mother, a widow with two sons both serving abroad in dangerous areas and who might, but for Beth, be left on her own. The need of both girls made the determination to survive very strong and was an important bond between them. 'Surely', they said to one another, 'daylight will come soon, and with it rescue, along with the other people in lifeboats. We shall see them and they will see us too, and we shall be comforted by that.'

Dawn came, the sky streaked easterly a dull yellow, scudding grey clouds rushed across the horizon, gales continued unabated. Such disappointment, though, as the girls, who had hoped to be able to see some sign of the others in lifeboats or on rafts, discovered that they were utterly alone, adrift on their upturned lifeboat in the middle of the Atlantic Ocean. The day wore on, fearsomely and remorselessly. It looked as if they would have to endure yet another night, becoming ever weaker and closer to death when, just as the sky began to cloud over with thick evening dusk, a small shape loomed on the horizon, becoming larger as it approached.

With incredulity, the girls realised that this moving object was a ship. As it came closer they realised that it was a Royal Navy destroyer – even a German ship would have been a welcome sight. HMS *Hurricane* was on its last sweep for survivors of the *City of Benares* before returning to its home port of Gourock. The crew had been picking up dead children and pitifully few survivors all day. Sighting the tiny lifeboat was a last miracle. Through salt-encrusted eyes, the girls watched a small boat being lowered from the ship's side and saw it being rowed closer and closer to them. The sailors for the *HMS Hurricane* rowing the ship's whaler managed, despite rough seas, to manoeuvre the boat close to the upturned lifeboat – a clever piece of seamanship. With the help of oil poured out of drums which they had stowed abroad, they obtained just enough surface tension to come alongside. They had to be very careful not to upturn the unstable lifeboat – if it had turned over in the water the girls would have been lost forever just at the point of rescue. The sailors hauled the girls and the seaman into the whaler and returned as fast as they could row to the destroyer.

On being carried aboard, the girls were received by the entire crew lined up on deck, cheering and crying unashamedly. These men had been in cold fury at the sight of so many dead children, and felt that to rescue two girls, barely alive, was a miracle. The Indian seaman rescued with them said that had it not been for the girls' determination to survive he would have given up the struggle. The children were carried gently below, exhausted, unable to speak, seriously dehydrated and salt-encrusted. They were bathed, their clothes cut away and wrapped in sheets and blankets. They were made comfortable and warm in the officers' cabins. The ship's young surgeon, Lieutenant Peter Collinson, cared for them like precious jewels and, with his assistants, gradually brought them to life again. Their clothes were taken down to the ships boiler room, where they hung on lines with the other survivors' clothing to dry.

There were only a few other survivors – among these, a young boy. Normally he would have revelled in the adventure of being on a warship but one terrible thought prevented this. He was deeply sad about the fate of his sister. He knew her survival was most unlikely. He had seen so many children drown – indeed his own rescue was a miracle. To cheer him up a kindly sailor took him on a tour of a ship. On reaching the boiler-room he spotted a bright green dressing gown hanging on a line. 'That's my sister's!' he cried. And the two children were reunited, incredibly happy to be with one another again. Just how fortunate they were had not yet been made known to them. Later they were told that only 13 children had been rescued by HMS Hurricane out of a total of 100 who had sailed.

Bess remembers Lt.Cdr.Simms visiting her in his cabin and telling her that he was taking his ship back to Scotland where she, her brother and Beth would be reunited with their parents. Because of their still-frail condition, both girls were taken off the destroyer by stretcher when the ship docked at Gourock. Once more the ship's crew paid them a moving tribute by lining the path to form an escort, raising their caps and giving them resounding cheers as they were lifted into the waiting ambulance. Then came the joyous reunion with their parents in Scotland. Bess' father had had to return to London to work but her mother, brother and Bess lived in part of a large Scottish mansion and she went to the local High School. The girls were visited in hospital by the destroyer's Commander and surgeon, where their parents were able to thank them personally for their miraculous rescue. Naturally enough, as they grew up, the girls remained friends. Even more firmly linked now, they are sisters-in-law! Bess married Beth's brother in 1947, the so the bond that began in mid-Atlantic in September 1940 remains as strong now as it was then.

Contributed by Barbara Webb

Blue Mandala by Rosie Gray

A Tale Of Two Giants

Once upon a time there was a giant who lived on a high hill in Manchester. The giant was so tall that when he stood on his tiptoes he could shove cats in the tops of trees. Sometimes he would reach up and grab a pigeon or two for his tea. Sometimes he would stand on a box and break off bits of cloud so he could stuff giant pillows or make fluffy balls to give to his glamorous giant girlfriend so she could remove her make-up at night. Sometimes, after he'd been eating feet soup or making fish dizzy-fish by stirring their ponds into whirlpools he would stand on some sturdy metal stepladders that he'd found in a skip in Sainsbury's car park and dry his hands on the sun.

One starry night the giant was sitting on the high hill with his glamorous giant girlfriend. They were holding hands and gazing into the night sky. The glamorous giant girlfriend sighed and said: "Ah, this is dead romantic, isn't it, Dave?" The giant said: "Aye." The glamorous giant girlfriend said: "You know, just you and me here, together, on this high hill in Manchester, under the bright moon and all them wonderful twinkling stars." And the giant said: "Aye." And the glamorous giant girlfriend said: "It's a great big mysterious mystery, isn't it, Dave?" And the giant said: "Aye." And the glamorous giant girlfriend said: "Wouldn't it be dead good if we could keep this moment forever? You know, just you and me, here on this high hill in Manchester under the bright moon and all them romantic, wonderful, twinkling, mysterious stars?" And the giant said: "Aye." The glamorous giant girlfriend thought for a while and then said: "Dave, you're tall, aren't you? Will you get me some of them stars?" The giant said: "Why?" The glamorous giant girlfriend said: "Well, you 'know ..." The giant said: "No, I don't." The glamorous giant girlfriend said: "So we can keep this romantic moment forever in our hearts, you silly person!" The giant said nothing. The glamorous giant girlfriend said: "Dave! Go on! If you love me, you'll reach up and get me some stars!" So the giant said: "Ok." He went away and then came back with a box and a giant bucket. He held the giant bucket carefully in his arms and as he was about to step on the box, the glamorous giant girlfriend said: "A bucket's no good, Dave! Twinkling stars won't look very nice in a bucket, will they?" The giant said nothing. Then the glamorous giant girlfriend said: "Anyway, choose some nice twinkly ones for me!" The giant stood on the box and reached upwards. He took a star from here and a star from there and a star from here and a star from there and soon he had picked a giant bucketful of twinkling stars. Then he got down and gave the giant bucketful of twinkling stars to the glamourous giant girlfriend. The glamorous giant girlfriend held the giant bucketful of twinkling stars and said "Aw, Ta, Dave! That's dead romantic, that is!" The giant said nothing and then the glamorous giant girlfriend said: "They are romantic though, aren't they, Dave?" The giant said: "Aye," and then sat down. They held hands. After a while the glamorous giant girlfriend said: "Dave, Dave, look at the bright moon. It's dead romantic isn't it?" The giant looked at the moon and said: "Aye." It went quiet and then the glamorous giant girlfriend said: Dave, Dave, will you get me that moon? It's dead romantic and we could put it in our bedroom and keep it forever so it reminds us of you and me, together here tonight, on this high hill in Manchester, under the bright moon and all them twinkling stars." The giant said: "Aye." He went away and came back with some sturdy metal stepladders that he'd found in a skip in Sainsbury's car park. He climbed up the stepladders and reached as high as he could to get the bright moon. The giant grasped the bright moon with both hands and carefully made his way down the stepladders. He gave the bright moon to the glamorous giant girlfriend who said: "Aw, thanks! That's dead romantic, that is, Dave!" It went quiet and then the glamorous giant girlfriend said: Dave, Dave, if you got me a piece of night sky I could make a pair of romantic black bedsheets and some black curtains and then it would be dead romantic forever, wouldn't it?" Then she said: "Wake up, Dave! Did you not hear what I just said? I want a piece of night sky, alright?" The giant said: "Aye." Then he got up and put the box on top of the sturdy metal stepladders that he'd found in a skip in Sainsbury's car park and climbed up on top of it. He swayed this way and he swayed that way, but in the end he managed to reach up and get hold of the night sky. He tore off a big piece and carefully made his way down the stepladder. Then he gave the big piece of night sky to the glamorous giant girlfriend who said" Aw, thanks, Dave – that's dead romantic!"

The next evening, the giant's bed had black night sky bed sheets on it and there were black night sky curtains on the windows twinkling stars on the ceiling and the bright moon high up on the wall. The glamorous giant girlfriend wiggled her giant toes under the bedsheets and looked up to the ceiling with its twinkling stars and over to the wall where the bright moon shone down and said: "Dave, Dave, I've made a wish under all them twinkling stars and bright moon. Do you want to make a wish, an' all?" The giant said nothing. The glamorous giant girlfriend wiggled her toes under the bedsheets and said: "Aw – go on, Dave! Make a wish! What do you really, really want on such a romantic evening like this?" The giant said nothing and then the glamorous giant girlfriend said: "Did you know, Dave that on such a romantic evening like this, wishes come true." The giant looked at her and said: "Aye?" The glamorous giant girlfriend looked at him and said: "Yes, Dave – a real gypsy told me. Go on, Dave - make a wish!" The giant smiled a big giant smile and then got out of bed. The glamorous giant girlfriend said: "Dave, Dave – where are you going?" The giant looked back over his shoulder and said: "Drinks!" The glamourous giant girlfriend wriggled her giant toes under the bedsheets and said: "Aw - will he bring me a giant bottle of *Salon Blanc de Blancs Le Mesnil-sur-Oger 1988* to complete the romance of this romantic evening?" The giant came back with a giant crate of industrial strength lager that he put by the side of the bed. The glamorous giant girlfriend said nothing and the giant got in bed. The glamorous giant girlfriend turned towards the giant and said: "Dave, have you made your wish yet?" The giant said: "Aye!" The glamorous giant girlfriend said: "Well, what was it - what did you wish for?" The giant got out of bed. The glamorous giant girlfriend pulled a giant face and said: "Dave, Dave – where are you going now?" The giant looked back over his shoulder and said: "Food." The glamorous giant girlfriend wriggled her giant toes under the bedsheets and said: "Aw - will he bring me grapes or chocolates or Turkish Delight to complete the romance of this romantic evening?" The giant came back with a giant plate full of giant pork pies that he put by the side of the bed. The glamorous giant girlfriend said nothing and the giant got in bed. The glamorous giant girlfriend said: "Dave, for heaven's sake will you dim them flamin' lights? We can't see them twinkling stars and bright moon in all their true mysterious mystery set against the romantic night sky curtains and these romantic night sky bedsheets with the lights on, can we?" The giant dimmed the lights. Then the giant looked at his watch and the glamorous giant girlfriend wriggled her giant toes under the bedsheets and said: "It's time, Dave! It's time to score!" The giant said: "Aye - at least three or four times!" The glamorous giant girlfriend smiled a big giant smile. The giant reached for the remote. The giant television screen lit up. The giant said: "We're playing Liverpool tonight and at this late stage of this - a most testing, and a surprisingly beleaguered season, it's vital that we secure every point possible. Relegation and its attendant existential, moral, reputational and financial consequences are simply unthinkable! Shall I pass you a can of sparkling lager and a pork pie or two, my precious love?"

Stephen Sayers

The Enchanter

'What *you* need boy is life experience!'

The words had an invigorating effect. Standing there in the classroom, the boy felt confident, powerful – adventurous; the world really could be his oyster.

'Seee that lott', continued the history master, waving through the window at departing sixth-formers. 'They'll go to Uni, get their 2.1s, sit through interminable internships at Nice Waterhouse...fall into comfortable civil service jobs. But they'll never experience real life.'

Victor Veritas was wasted at a provincial school – so people said. 'D Phil Oxon' – he'd probably always intended Brightwell Comprehensive as a stepping stone. So it was no surprise to young Oliver, when Victor announced he was leaving at the end of the year. The two of them would be on the same leavers photograph!

Oliver Dilettante was – in his own words – 'a cocky bugger.' Big – tall that is, not the obese kind – grinning and ginger. Good at getting himself noticed. Clever, he knew it, the teachers knew it. Always first in the queue for things he wanted, last for things he didn't. He had an answer for everything.

Oliver's dad worked for the post office - Mum a dinner lady, but however much he loved them, nobody quite matched up to 'Victor.'

Veritas's teaching style was mature – that was you had to be mature-minded to benefit from it...No 'learning by heart', no 'drumming in'. It was what Oliver thought it must be like being at Uni – having a proper lecture.

Veritas talked, walked about the classroom. He never used blackboard, whiteboard; flipcharts. It didn't make any difference whether he was talking about the '9th Thermidor,' or the 'Long Parliament', if he wanted emphasis he would move closer to his audience.

The sensation of having Veritas's head – rather like a carnival head - floating inches away from one's own - the lips flabby and moist with mounting excitement, the nose, hooked and emperor-like - was more than sufficient to indelibly imprint upon ones mind the actions of Marat, or Robespierre.

Head and hair gave the impression of two elements hopelessly incompatible with one another. The slate-hued hair worn in a shaggy fringe made him look like a fancy-dress party-goer topped with an ill-fitting wig. It was pure drama.

That summer, the school had arranged a theatre outing, and instead of the traditional proscenium arch, it had been theatre in the round – audience sitting on all four sides of the stage. Magical, thought Oliver - and here was Veritas continuing that vision in the form of his own history lessons.

Oliver lost no opportunity to seek his pedagogue's approval... Felt superior to other boys so never bothered to make friends. He wanted to be Veritas's friend, but the man was twenty years his senior so why should he be?

'Why are you al'a's "pashin' up" to Owd Victor?' sneered young Netherwood. 'E could be one a 'them' ya know. Look 'ow close 'e comes with 'is ugly mug; gives me the effin' creeps.'

Netherwood was clearly jealous, and incapable of recognizing genius when he saw it. Oliver longed for some kind of sign that Veritas approved of him.

Then came the official leavers photograph, and by luck Oliver found himself on the front row right next to the great master who sat in the centre of the composition, the only departing teacher that year. There they were, comrades, and both destined for great things.

Oliver had already decided that he wouldn't apply for university, and when October came he travelled to London to stay with his uncle in Walthamstow. He was excited by the New Wave music he heard, became friends with members of bands, had notions of being a pop impresario; but it was no more than a vague vision.

Oliver thought a lot about Veritas. Rumour had it that he'd been given a lectureship at his old Oxford College – Regents Park. Oliver even thought of going to see him. Then he had an idea. He'd been going to a lot of fringe theatre, he would become an actor!

He selected a well-known company, ingratiated himself with the director – got an audition! This was it. It was what he knew he did best in life, being centre stage, making people want him, forcing them to like him.

'Take three months over it', said the director. 'Then come back and give me three monologues; we'll take it from there'.

It was the longest twelve weeks Oliver had known. He learned the lines within a week – easy! Pheobe, his uncle's partner offered him advice.

'Never produce more than one well-known speech, that way a director has a better opportunity to recognize your ability to communicate'. Oliver didn't see it that way at all. Shakespeare was a must – Hamlet it had to be, Oscar Wilde his comic relief...and of course, Chekhov.

What to wear? Phoebe suggested a suit.

'When you're established, they'll want you to go fund raising – charity events and the like, you've gotta look the part...Show you're flexible – that you can be anybody'. Oliver knew all that; not a bit of it, he was going to wear his baggiest pirate shirt, tightest bum-hugging jeans, and a hat. An actor had to have a hat.

On the day it was just the two of them, Oliver, and the director who sat well back in the auditorium. The boy stood on the stage under a spotlight. There was a strong smell of patchouli. Oliver heard the buzzer go, and after a short pause he began;

'Why does your aunt call you her uncle?...' the buzzer sounded. What! He obviously didn't reckon much to his *The Importance of Being Earnest.* Oliver turned his back to the director.

'Bzzzz,' Slowly Oliver turned to face his audience. The fug of patchouli was sending dangerous signals through sinuses and down nostrils. This was Oliver's great moment. Stretching out both arms he cried

'*What a piece of work is a man!...*' He failed to get any further. The compulsion to sneeze caused the lower part of his face to distort. Top lip forcing itself to cover upper front teeth, so what actually emerged was,

'What a piece of work is a Mam!'

Oliver waited for the buzzer. It did not sound. The bastard! He was going to see how he would deal with his misfortune. Oliver had a wild idea. Tuesdays with Mummy was a crazy farce by Wade Bradford about fishmonger Rigby Neville who just happens to have the same name as the renowned Egyptologist, and is mistakenly packed off to investigate the tomb of Thutmes the Third. Oliver had just been to see it and had memorized the principle monologue.

It was a brilliant piece of quick-thinking to turn one of Hamlet's key speeches into a humorous preface. He could almost feel the director smiling at him in the darkness, as he let him run to his full two minutes.

Then it was Chekhov's *The Seagull.* Again Oliver faced away from the auditorium, and when he turned round he was Treplev.

'She loves me – she loves me not....*she loves me – she loves me not*....this time the sneeze came, and with such force that if Oliver had been wearing false teeth, they would have shot onto the boards. Treplev is supposed to laugh at this point, but what the hell, thought Oliver.

'There you are – She doesn't love me......' It was a dramatic tour de force.

'Okay, I don't see people every day so give me another three months to think about it, and I'll let you know.' Oliver was crestfallen.

Back in his bedroom in Walthamstow, he decided to write to Veritas.

Dear Victor – yes Victor it had to be. After all they were comrades in 'the school of life' now.

Dear Victor

I feel that I am at a crossroads....

Oliver hoped that life was treating him well in Oxford.... then he played his trump card.

Since - what he saw as - his unmitigated success at the audition, and the director's miserable response, he'd decided that if he didn't hear from the man within three months, he would join the police force. It would be part self-inflicted punishment for his failure to win a job in the theatre, yet it would be character building - like national service.

There would be dedication, the saving of lives, helping people restart their cars, handcuffing paedophiles and rapists, delivering the odd baby, and of course the danger. Veritas would be bound to write back in order to save him;

'For God's sake boy, don't do it!'

Fatalistically he booked the police interview for the week following the end of the three month period. The day arrived there was no word from the director, and worse still nothing from Veritas. Along he went, was offered a job - constable with the London Met.

The day the job offer from the theatre arrived, Oliver was on a course, learning riot control tactics. It stood him in good stead as he soon found himself on duty in central London during a night of disturbances...Students protesting about government cuts to grants. There was a stand-off.

By dusk many of the demonstrators had disbursed, leaving a hardcore of moody-looking anarchists. Protestors were advancing, pushing back police - then the officers rallied. Oliver noticed a figure behind the line – alone, and standing atop a flight of steps. He broke away to take a closer look, raised his visor as the smoke cleared. It was Veritas...

...Unmistakable in the street light. Bareheaded, and with a long wool scarf wrapped around his neck, the mop top - though longer - plastered to cranium. There was something monumental about his appearance, brutish, fascistic. He looked like a general directing his troops. A Molotov cocktail flared and as Oliver gazed, the large emperor-like head turned, hook nose profiled in the glare, chin cloven like the hoof of some wild beast. The mouth opened, as if to say something; it sounded like 'Pig!'

'You're a troublemaker Dilettante, aren't you?' said the Chief, pop-of-eye, square-of-head, and moustache – a perfect half circle of hair the colour of used bath water.

'No sir!' insisted Oliver.

The Chief slapped his sapele-veneered desk. 'Some of our chaps were injured in that riot and you knew the ringleader! He denied having ever set eyes on you, but PC Boyce claims there was no doubt that you knew him.'

There was nothing else for it. Oliver jumped before he was pushed.

Dear Victor

I have decided to enter the priesthood...

He had so wanted to mention the fearful scene that night near Regent Street to mitigate for himself; explain that he was only doing his duty - acting on the man's advice by enlisting for the 'school of hard knocks.' Instead he unfolded his plan to become ordained.

Why not? God was looking for folk who had charisma - searching for unique and distinctive people capable of nurturing a vision, and upholding a loving mission to the world. There seemed to be something Faustian about the way his career was unfolding. One smartarse at the DDO Ordinands interview asked him if he was deliberately trying to work his way through the Humanities. There was no word from Veritas.

One night Oliver was watching television, when Veritas appeared on the screen. Head still Roman emperor-like, but with a more benign Augustinian look than on the last occasion Oliver had seen him. It seemed that the guru had published a book entitled The Future of the Past - a philosophical work. Oliver obtained reviews.

Criticism appeared to be grouping itself into three camps; those who hailed it as '*a radical link between the existentialist and the theological,*' others who saw it as '*a Utopian metaphor*', and a third minority who felt it was '*a calculated manipulation of British agnostics.*' Willard Widgery of the magazine *Spiritual Positivism* risked his career by referring to it as '*a load of pretentious crap*'!

Oliver felt hurt that Veritas had failed to answer his letters. The two men had a common bond. Veritas might be the established academic, the elevated man of learning, but Oliver had heeded the call to adventure, had followed the advice of his teacher, no one could deny that. Yet the months continued to pass in silence.

He heard the great man's voice on *Twenty Questions,* and it was even rumoured that he had gone to the US - an exchange with Harvard. Oliver's mother furnished him with newspaper cuttings from the local provincial press featuring articles on the sage who still visited the town, staying in the house once owned by his now-deceased parents.

It was a long hard road which Oliver had trodden, but the day arrived when he received his ordination, and as luck would have it, a parish, close to his old home town. One sermon a week; one service a day were by no means using all his energies. He developed an interest in the occult. He'd become familiar with the darker sides of life whilst in the police force, and after all, if one was a servant of God, and had the responsibility of leading folk in worship, then it could only be beneficial to give oneself an idea about what 'the other side' was up to.

He read that Veritas had published a sequel to *The Future of the Past*, under the title *The Past of the Future.* Oliver wrote to congratulate him but still no reply came.

He tried his hand at novel writing - within the genre of the supernatural, and raising eyebrows at the diocesan office when his first novel received publication. He even made plans to leave The Church for a full time writing career.

News reached Oliver that Veritas was planning to visit his home town and would be - he assumed - staying at his parent's old house. He decided to pay him a visit.

It was an evening in late October; the air was dry and there was a scent of garden fires mixed with the smell of early fireworks. Oliver parked his car under a street light, and walked noiselessly on the concrete paving slabs, his black cassock gently swaying from side to side.

As if by magic, and standing motionless under the next streetlight, was Veritas. That head - unmistakable, but what a contrast to the terrible night near Regent Street! Standing by an immaculately-mown suburban lawn, and dressed in an anorak, he looked oddly dull.

The two men stood and stared, examining one another like forensic scientists. As their gazes met, a look of pure disgust appeared in Veritas's eyes. The lips pursed. In the street lamp they glistened like a monstrous sea anemone, exposed and clinging to a rock after the water has sucked itself away. The mouth opened, the words came spitting out.

'The trouble with you boy, is that you could never stick at anything!' The mouth clamped shut.

Surely it was some kind of a joke – it had to be!

As truth dawned Oliver felt white heat, saw white light. His cassock-clad arms shot forward, hands grabbed the hood of Veritas's anorak and shook it. Oliver's dog collar burst away from his neck with the effort of shaking. The pedagogue's head begin to wobble - its coarse salt and pepper hair sticking out at angles. As Oliver's hands rocked back and forth the great head resembled a giant coconut – an unwelcome prize won in some hellish fairground. Oliver broke free, and with his hands covering his mouth he ran, almost tripping over his cassock.

'Local Philosopher Dies' read the headline in the local paper.

At first Oliver thought it might have been his fault. The great man was only sixty eight...A heart attack...High blood pressure – it could have happened any time. Local tributes were fulsome;

'Home Grown Great, a man ahead of his time'.

Oliver bought a Telegraph...A short obituary, and as he

sat at his kitchen table, he felt anticipation so intense, as to be close to fever. Veritas might be dead but at last he, Oliver, could be alone with the great master for those few precious moments which had been denied to him all these years.

'Victor Veritas, A Master of Deception:

Veritas – whose real name was John Smith – fooled the academic world for almost half a century. He first earned notoriety at Regents Park College - not as the Oxford Don most believed him to be but - as a regular gate-crasher at lectures and tutorials. He was briefly employed by the college as a janitor. His only association with Harvard was his forced removal – following an incident of heckling – from a lecture entitled *Existentialism - a Return to Humanity,* and given by Darryl H Gravitas. The act of publishing a philosophical work –*The Future of the Past,* only to succeed it a few months later with The Past of the Future – a book which blow-by-blow deconstructed the original thesis - was considered an insult to those who had so fervently upheld the substance of the first work. The BBC and Channel 4 rejoiced in 'Veritas's inflammatory views and he was a frequent recipient of media invitations. Even his D Phil Oxon was a fake. Veritatem Dies Aperit (Time reveals the Truth).'

Oliver put both his cassock-clad elbows on the table, his ginger head fell into his hands, and he sobbed. He – more than most it seemed - would miss him.

If only the man could have answered just one of his letters...

John Fieldhouse

Mandala by Rosie Gray

Paving Over England

This garden gives notice of its closure due to re-location.
We apologise for any inconvenience this may cause.

When we've rolled up our grass, moss, fallen leaves,
half-eaten apples, sodden remains of autumn colchicums,
moth larvae, earwigs, the deflated World Cup football,
firework sticks, iris seed heads, over-blown iceberg roses,
and we've tucked in the un-trimmed edges, we'll vamoose.
We expect that the blackbirds, hedge sparrows, bluetits
will follow, in their own self-interest. Their little heads
may not be troubled by a sense of your betrayal,
but they must eat. So goodbye. We hope you'll enjoy
the concrete under the wobbly legs of your
brand new patio set and you won't fret too much
when the rains come and the street floods. No regrets.

Helen Cadbury

Gruff

Gruff. Good dog. Good. Good dog. Doggy dog. Good. Me. That's me. Who? What? Where was I? Chasing rabbits one minute and now? Oh yes. Back here again. Looking around...it's that...it's that ...oh what d'you call it? Here I am, back in that place, is it that theatre? I can't quite tell. One minute, I'm lounging about in dog heaven, next minute I get a call. You did call, didn't you? Thought so, always come when I'm called, good dog, pat on the head, scratch behind the ears, ooh, lovely. Mind if I sniff your hand?

Ah! Humans, my favourite smell. Oh, don't worry, don't be afraid, I don't bite. Well brought up dog, me. Well dragged up pup, oh yes. Me mam was a real lady, a prima donna. Know what that means? It means a leading lady, and so she was. A lady amongst mongrels: a pearl amongst swine. A jewel amongst dogs. A performer, you know. She trod the boards. Those very boards that are just through those doors, across the way, or they were, it looks different now. Looks like they've had the builders in.

I'd hardly know the place. You'll have to trust me, somewhere, not so far from here, was the stage. Picture the scene, a hundred and twenty years ago. It's variety night. Lots of different acts, singers and funny men, dancers, and funny women too. Sometimes the funny men dressed up as funny women and the funny women dressed up as funny men. It was funny. Other animals dressed as clowns or babies, and of course, there was always a performing dog. That was my mother. She was one of the best, at the top of her profession. She performed alongside a comic whose name was Sir Archibald Boomish Bombastic. A large gentlemen, prone to sweating. His was a song and dance act, with jokes in between. He sang, mam danced. Then, for his finale, he threw a ball in the air and she caught it on her nose and balanced it there. After a few moments, she flicked it up high, with a toss of her head. The crowd gasped. Her mouth opened wide and she caught it, perfect, every time. You want to know the secret of Sir Archibald

Boomish Bombastic's success? Simple. The ball was coated in meat paste and my mam loved it. Her reward was to lick the ball clean. Yum, yum, yum. And as she was kept on very short rations, she was always hungry and happy to do as she was asked.

A night here, a night there, Sir Archibald and my mother toured the land, well Yorkshire, with the occasional foray to the seaside resorts of Lancashire. I like a good foray, don't you? A journey, a hunt. Sir Archie went in search of fame and fortune, mam went for a lick of meat paste and the occasional marrowbone, if ticket sales were good. But the trick always worked better when she was hungry. Are you hungry? D'you want my advice? If you're hungry get a pie. A nice meaty pie. Ignore the crust, just go for the inside. Oh, my mouth's watering just to think of it. Sorry. Where was I? Me mam. Well, she'd done Scarborough, she'd done Filey, she'd done a night at the new Spa Theatre at Bridlington. You been? Very nice spot. That fresh sea air gets this city smoke out of your throat and lungs. Then, joy of joys, Sir Archibald Boomish Bombastic was offered a night right here in York, number five on the bill, him and his songs, and mam and her dancing and her tricks. You might not think number five sounds very good but I'll have you know there were ten acts on that bill. It was a night of variety. Ten acts of the highest quality, well, mostly. I'm not sure about the Peking Fan Dancers, there was a rumour they came from Macclesfield, not China, but that's neither here nor there. My point is that number five is half way to the top if you're on a bill of ten. Half way up. Not half way down.

Well, Sir Archibald and Mam, here they are in York. Quite a fancy crowd that night, you can't hear yourself think for the rustling of silks and the creaking of whalebone corsets (we dogs have very sharp hearing). And the smells! Can you imagine? Mam's thinking that some of these coves and their ladies could do with a visit to the bathhouse or a dip in the Ouse. They've doused themselves in cologne and lavender water but it's not doing much good in the heat of the auditorium. Beyond the flare of the lime-lights, she can see their heads bobbing. They're smiling and laughing. They're loving old Archibald's songs. They clap when she does her first little dance. And she's such a very pretty dog, my mother. Big dark eyes and long black lashes that some of those ladies in the audience would give their eye teeth for. Those that still have any teeth. And she's got one ear more up, it's more perky than the other, so that when he asks her a question, she cocks her head on one side. He says 'Now then, Princess,' and she looks at him, as if to say: 'Now, then, Mr Bombsatic, what's it to be?' She never calls him Sir, because he's never actually been knighted by Queen Victoria herself or anyone else for that matter, and Mam's very strict on matters of decorum. But her look is very quizzical. It's a 'what?' Or a 'how?' Or a 'what's the deal here' kind of look. And he's getting ready to throw the ball and he's doing a bit of patter, a bit of banter and the audience are watching and waiting and the ball flies up and there's an ooh and an ah, and it lands and she's balancing it on top of her nose. And this night, this particular night in York, when Sir Archibald Boomish Bombastic has worked his way up to the number five spot and he can't believe his luck, that ball just teeters there for a moment, on Ma's nose, and the next thing will be the flick of the head and the ball will fly up into the air. But something's amiss, not quite right. There's something fishy here. Her nose twitches, her head flicks, the ball goes up. But instead of opening her mouth for the catch, she lets it fall, lets it drop, with a thump on the stage, and down it rolls to the orchestra pit where it hits a bald violinist smack on the head.

"What you doing?' mutters Archie, 'What in the name of tarnation are you doing?'

She looks at him. Doesn't he know? Instead of meat paste, in all his haste and nerves, he's only smeared it with fish paste instead. Well, all hell breaks loose. The violinist is standing up on his chair, hauling himself out of the orchestra pit and onto the stage. As he drags himself between two footlights, his coat catches a spark and he's on fire. The audience think it's part of the act. They're roaring and cheering, and egging him on. But Mam knows, she knows it's all going terribly wrong. She's barking, the two men are shouting, someone comes on from the wings with a bucket of water, throws, misses the violinist and hits Mam instead, more laughter. The curtains close, to applause and whistles and catcalls. Sir Archibald Boomish Bombastic is bright red in the face, he picks up his stick, a solid affair with a silver tip and comes at my mam, calling her all the bad names he can think of and he gives her a terrible whack.

Suddenly three big stage-hands are there, two of them throw a blanket over the burning man and roll him on the floor and the other one, the biggest one of all, grabs Sir Archie's stick and breaks it over his knee and tells old Archie to shove off and never darken the doors of this theatre again. Mam's whimpering from being whacked and shivering from having water thrown on her and this big feller picks her up in his strong arms and whispers in her ear: *'Don't worry princess, you'll be safe with Bill.'*

It all calms down and the show resumes with the Peking Fan Dancers from Macclesfield. Mam is backstage with her hero, Bill; her knight in shining armour. He used to work on a whaler out of Grimsby, and now he works the ropes that fly the scenery in and out. He makes her a bed in a little lean-to shed where they keep the spare kit. And there she stays, and in time, she meets a gentleman dog, my father, and then I'm born and I stay there too. Mam never goes on stage again, her dancing days are over. The incident with the fish paste and the ball and the burning violinist (who was perfectly unharmed, he just lost a very nice tailcoat) has put her off, she says, but she tells me stories until late into the night. And when she is an old dog, she falls asleep as old dogs do, and never wakes up again.

I miss her very much and so does Bill. He buries her in the little graveyard up the road a bit behind the theatre. And in time, I join her there. So, you ask, because you are a very clever and attentive person, how am I telling you this story if I'm a dead dog? How indeed. Now don't be afraid, don't scared. The garden is no more. It was built on and built over and then what was there was knocked down and dug out. And when they were digging they found some bones. What a fuss and racket! Are they Roman or medieval? What piece of history are they from? The best archaeologists in the city were called upon and when they put their glasses on, they said, oh, no, these are nothing important, just dog's bones, Victorian probably. Three dogs, laid to rest some years apart, next to one other. Good old Bill.

Helen Cadbury

Tomte and Squirrel Friend by Brenda Tyler